T0115181

# THE

# Archangel Michael

## —— EXPERIMENT ——

## A 30-day adventure into knowing

### Debra Walker

**BALBOA.**
PRESS

A DIVISION OF HAY HOUSE

ISBN: 978-1-4525-5492-1 (sc)
ISBN: 978-1-4525-5493-8 (e)

Balboa Press books may be ordered through booksellers or by contacting:

Balboa Press
A Division of Hay House
1663 Liberty Drive
Bloomington, IN 47403
www.balboapress.com
1-(877) 407-4847

Because of the dynamic nature of the Internet, any web addresses or
links contained in this book may have changed since publication and
may no longer be valid. The views expressed in this work are solely those
of the author and do not necessarily reflect the views of the publisher,
and the publisher hereby disclaims any responsibility for them.

The author of this book does not dispense medical advice or prescribe the use
of any technique as a form of treatment for physical, emotional, or medical
problems without the advice of a physician, either directly or indirectly. The
intent of the author is only to offer information of a general nature to help
you in your quest for emotional and spiritual well-being. In the event you use
any of the information in this book for yourself, which is your constitutional
right, the author and the publisher assume no responsibility for your actions.

Any people depicted in stock imagery provided by Thinkstock are
models, and such images are being used for illustrative purposes only.
Certain stock imagery © Thinkstock.

Printed in the United States of America
Balboa Press rev. date: 07/23/12

This book is dedicated to the extraordinary women in my family, who show me what it means to truly shine.

# Foreword

I AM DELIGHTED TO write the foreword for this book. Debra Walker is not only my Mom, but the best friend a daughter could have. For as long as I can remember she has always viewed life in an unconventional way. She is always reaching for more and exploring possibilities to help improve her quality of life, and be an inspiration to others as well.

Through her own life experiences, she has come to understand how important it is to direct your thoughts in a positive, intentional way to achieve what you desire.

I am thankful for this experience, not only for the way it has touched my mother's life, but for all of the wonderful insights I have gotten while being a part of it. I hope this book finds you with an open mind, and a light heart.

Enjoy!
Casey Warner

# Preface

Everyone experiences issues concerning relationships, prosperity, empowerment, even well-being in general. It doesn't matter who you are or how much you know, it is a part of life. There are many ways to seek solutions to those issues. It just so happens that I was compelled to take a rather unconventional approach to mine. As a result, I can say it has been the best thing I have ever done.

What you are about to discover, is the reason I chose this different approach and how it worked for me. This truly was an experiment to see if what I felt encouraged and inspired to do would help transform my life in the ways I had hoped for.

What you are about to read is the daily accounting of my experiences with Michael as a personal guide to that transformation. It has always been a habit of mine to write down insights, ideas, amazing experiences, and anything that feels important to me. So naturally, I wrote down my 30 day experience with Michael. How I was impacted, what it was like and what I took away from it. As you will see, turns out it is a good thing I did.

From day one it was apparent I would have to stay out of my own way. I knew from the start that I would have to maintain a relaxed state of trust and allowing to receive the greatest benefit from this experience. Although some days were trickier than others, I managed to remain true to it until the end. I know it was a big factor in how well this went and why I received so much from it.

I did my best to describe what it was like to experience what I can only say was a blending with Michael. The way it felt to be aligned with Michael's powerful knowing was nothing short of incredible. From the many books I have read about interacting with the non-physical, no one really explains a lot about what it feels like. Yet that was probably one of the most amazing aspects of this.

Without question, the most challenging part was finding the words that could accurately describe the knowing I had received. But I'm sure Michael even helped me with that. The best part is that Michael brilliantly addressed every issue in ways that anyone can understand and benefit from.

I consider this to be a down to earth, deceptively simple, master course on how to create the life you want. I wouldn't have expected anything less from Michael. I hope you enjoy the journey.

# Introduction

I HAVE HEARD THAT when you are asking to transform your life, there is a good chance all hell will break loose first. That is exactly what seems to have happened now that I am seeing all of the ways my life isn't working anymore.

My partnership has become a point of contention (to say the least), finances are as up and down as a carnival ride, and frankly I know I could and should be a whole lot happier. I know about the law of attraction and that we create our own reality, I get that. But knowing it in theory and actually putting into practice by living it is another story.

So I came to the conclusion I am in need of a little divine intervention to bridge that gap. I have been meditating daily for the last couple of months to regain some balance and I think there is a connection between that and coming up with this plan. Which leads me to Archangel Michael……..

I have a history with Michael that began years ago during a particularly challenging time in my life. I have always been very sensitive and didn't really know much about energy, much less how it affected me. It felt like I was vulnerable to any negativity that came into my vicinity. It even got to the point that I experienced more and more anxiety as well as frequent nightmares.

That is about the time I knew I needed some kind of understanding and help. It came for me one day when I decided to go to this little religious shop and ask what helped with fears and protection. I was told Archangel Michael. I purchased an Archangel Michael medallion and when I got to my car, as I put it around my neck I was instantly filled with tingling sensations and goose bumps throughout my body. I felt an ease come over me as if things were going to get better, and they did.

Through the years since then, I have asked for Michael's help countless times when things got tough and help has come through in one way or another every time. So who better than Michael to help me out now? I have this whole idea come to me as sort of an experimental co-creative journey that would be beyond anything I have ever experienced, and be exactly what I need.

I decide to ask Michael to spend 30 days with me to guide me through what I need to know and understand to turn my life around. I get an incredibly good feeling come over me and I know I am about to set out on a potentially life changing adventure.

# Day 1                    *March 13, 2011*

I AM BEYOND EAGER and excited to begin this journey with Michael. As I acknowledge my intention to begin, I instantly experience the strong buzzing sensations and good feeling vibrations I have become accustomed to when I am in alignment, tuned in and beautifully connected.

The only way to really describe it is like that vibration sound a hummingbird makes with its wings. Imagine that buzzing sound right next to your head, circling around and around so closely, it feels as if it is almost part of you. From years of doing energy work it has become a physical indication of being on the same wavelength as the non-physical or what I refer to as the larger part of me. Basically it is my confirmation that Michael is on board and ready to begin as well.

Right away it occurs to me that getting hung up on any particular ideas of preconceptions about how this is going to play out would be completely counter-productive. I definitely feel that Michael is encouraging me to stay out of my busy little mind on this. Implying that over thinking it would not allow for the possibilities and expansive experience otherwise available to me. Knowing me, that is the best advice I could receive as I set out on this co- creative endeavor. Actually, come to think of it, that is just plain good advice for anything.

Before long, it is feeling like that is enough for starters as I am sensing we will be easing into this until I get my "sea legs" so to speak. As the day winds to a close, I decide to ask Michael to help me with feeling comfortable enough to ask for WHATEVER I want. I do not want to impose any restrictions on myself or this experience—then I feel an ease come over me; I take that as a yes.

# Day 2             *March 14, 2011*

IT IS EARLY MORNING on this second day and I am already feeling better and more optimistic than I have in a while. I feel Michael's presence in a different way than before. It feels like coming together in a partnership with a plan that has already been formulated on my behalf and ready to be executed. Even so, I decide to write down what feels most important to me at the moment (my partnership issue) as my way of getting the ball rolling, since I am in uncharted territory here. That is the beauty of this; it makes for a great exercise in trust, possibility and adventure.

I am also hoping to enhance and expand my ability to interact with the non-physical. I believe it is not only of great benefit to us, but our natural birthright. To tell you the truth, I would love to milk this for all it's worth!

It is later in the day and a clear understanding has come to me regarding my partnership. I am seeing that my struggling and trying too hard, focusing so much attention on trying to fix it, has only kept me feeling frustrated and powerless.

I have been making it too much about him. I have been putting so much thought into all of the ways he could or should be doing things so I will feel better. It is like I am being given an aerial view of myself going through hoops and running in circles trying to do the impossible, which frankly is just wearing me out.

Then like lights coming on in a stadium, my moment of clarity.... "nobody is a big player in my life except me". As a matter of fact, I am the only player that really counts. Oh boy, that would mean somehow I have come to believe that somebody else is responsible for and holds the power over how I feel. Well it's no wonder all of this has made me feel powerless, now I clearly see that is simply not true. What a friggin relief! It literally feels like a burden has been lifted with that simple yet powerful perspective from Michael......oh happy day!

# Day 3                                    *March 15, 2011*

LAST NIGHT AS I was sitting here, I felt a little overwhelmed, and started to feel those all too familiar feelings of frustration I had before I began this journey. All I could think about was how much I didn't want to feel that way anymore. Before I knew it, there was a sensation in my back area that felt like a strong energy pushing something inside of me. I instinctively knew Michael was working on something and have learned not to try and question these experiences; it is just not possible to know what is really going on. It didn't last too long, and as it let up I felt a wonderful sense of trust and ease come over me. I could feel that all is well.

This morning it is immediately obvious that Michael must have activated something with that energy experience because I am feeling like I have tapped into a momentum of sorts. It is like a door has opened and I am receiving thoughts infused with understanding in a significantly more powerful, uplifting way. It feels like clear guidance with an undeniable sense of knowing that somehow translates into words that I can relate to. And the message is clear; my mindset is the key to self-empowerment.

It comes to me that I can and in fact am always defining who I am. Therefore deciding how I choose to see myself. Then it comes in the form of a question as if Michael was asking it. How do I see myself? Letting me know that as I claim myself to be, that is what I will experience. And that my perception of myself, or anything else for that matter, is a direct result of what I chose to think or believe.

I can create my life to be the way I want. I can choose my thoughts deliberately toward what I prefer and get what I want. Or I can allow my thoughts to run amuck and let my experiences be a reflection of that. This is not a new idea, but receiving it from Michael's powerful vantage point; I now understand that I am the creator of my life. On one hand it is a scary thought, but on the other it is completely empowering.

# Day 4                                 *March 16, 2011*

It seems like the perfect timing for my daughter and delightful little granddaughter's to come for a visit today. What a great way to allow my experiences so far to settle in and spend some time with what I consider to be some of the best little teachers on the planet. There is something almost magical about being around these little ones with the way they welcome me into their wonderful world, enabling me to grant myself permission to join them in their un-inhibited enthusiasm for life.

What a lovely ride it is as they remind me to play, explore, and just have fun. They are such truly great examples of how to spontaneously and fearlessly live in the moment. I will never forget the story my daughter told me about my 3 year old granddaughter.

She had written a note especially for her mommy and gave it to her. It was just scribbles, but my daughter being the great mom that she is asked what it said. With a look of certainty in her eyes she replied "believe your heart and don't give up". Tell me, does it get any better than that?

I can honestly say that I have learned more about how to be who I truly am from these little girls than anything else. What a blessing and such a great way to enhance my life even more right now.

# Day 5        *March 17, 2011*

PICKING UP RIGHT WHERE we left off before the girls visit, I return my awareness to the importance of my mindset. All I want to do is snuff out all of the detrimental thoughts that are keeping me from what I want, to get rid of them and the sooner the better. My automatic response is to initiate damage control so everything can start getting better.

So off I go into a monologue with Michael about how I need help releasing all of this stuff so I can achieve the mindset that I prefer. I think I am pleading a pretty good case about why I need help when something interesting happens. It suddenly occurs to me that I may be taking the wrong approach here. This idea that I need to get rid of obstacles that are holding me back in order to get what I want, is feeling off to me.

Maybe it is the idea of reaching this goal SOMEDAY after I have eliminated all of the problems, which is actually the problem here. It's like being in a hurry to get somewhere and getting irritated because some slow poke is in my way. Then I finally get around them and there is another one right there to take their place. The more I want these road turtles out of my way, the more they show up and my destination seems to fall further out of reach.

No sooner do I get this clarity, Michael comes in with the goods….. it's about right now; claiming it for myself now, being it now, acting as though I am there until I have convinced myself of it. The quickest way to be there is to feel that you are already there. What a beautiful way to bridge and reinforce the previous message "as you claim yourself to be, you will be". I love how patiently Michael waits for me to come to my senses and allow what is so graciously given. It reinforces the fact that I can relax and trust this process completely.

# Day 6 *March 18, 2011*

I AM REALLY GETTING into a greater ease and flow with Michael's interaction and guidance now. It is beginning to feel more like hanging out with one of the best friends I could ever have. Don't even get me started about how it has rocked my perceptions regarding the non-physical, particularly my ideas of what an archangel might be. I can honestly say that I cannot define it anymore now than before, but it sure isn't what most of us think.

It is more expansive than we can even get our minds wrapped around. Any ideas I have had about there being some more advanced hierarchy have simply been replaced with a feeling of equality, and I will just leave it at that. At this point, I especially love that my every thought or intention is not only completely understood, but being addressed in the best possible way.

This is such an interesting blend of a dynamic inspirational awareness coming in a down to earth, matter of fact way. An interaction based on a mutual intention between Michael and I providing an experience I have always imagined was possible. Being able to interact with the larger part of us that is very real but simply existing on a different (vibrational) level than we are in our physical experience.

I have always felt that there could be a real benefit and enjoyment from having access to more than we are receiving from everything around us. That there is more to know and understand that would help us have an even greater, more expanded, and ultimately more fulfilling life experience. I must say, I have already had some pretty amazing experiences with some of the energy work that I have done. I have had many moments of clarity, guidance and healing from those experiences, still this little adventure with Michael is taking everything to a whole new level. I would highly recommend it.

# Day 7 *March 19, 2011*

FOR QUITE SOME TIME I have been feeling a void inside of me as if I am living a limited version of myself, my life. It feels like there is so much creativity, ability and untapped potential within me wanting to be expressed, but getting suppressed instead. Maybe I have spent so much time and energy trying to manage everything other than what I want, that I have become my last priority.

It is pretty easy to get in the habit of taking care of everything else and begin settling for less and less for yourself. Before you know it, you have completely lost touch with your passion, dreams, and purpose. That is exactly what I am addressing with Michael today. Technically Michael is responsible for lighting this fire under my butt, causing me to feel like a kid turned loose in a candy store with all that I want within my reach. And I want it all!

I want the financial independence, the wonderful relationship, and to use my talents and abilities in ways that are satisfying and rewarding. Most importantly, I want to live the joyful happy life that I deserve. This experience is so uplifting and inspiring; it's like letting the Genie out of the bottle. Maybe that is the point.

Later in the afternoon as I am out on my walk, Michael is encouraging me to be open minded about the direction I have asked for. Michael is letting me know that the more open I am, the greater the benefit for me. After I return home and check my email, there is one from Hay House Publishing about a self-publishing division they have created for new Authors, called Balboa Press. For a moment I wonder if Michael is trying to show me something because I haven't made any contact that would cause me to receive this information. Since I don't believe in coincidence it has me a bit intrigued. I figure that what I want or need, will become completely evident sooner or later, and I am more than satisfied with trusting that Michael will come through.

# Day 8                    *March 20, 2011*

I HAVE ALWAYS FELT a sense of sacredness and symbolism with the spring equinox. Even more so today being on this journey with Michael as spring arrives. I have a friend that has always said there is nothing by chance, and it definitely seems that it is not by chance I am having this experience at this time.

I am one of those curious types that love to see how things are connected and play out in our lives. I have got to say that this experience has already made me more acutely aware of the deeper meaning and value in almost everything. It is like my senses have been heightened and my perception and understanding of everything has expanded. Like I have been looking at life through binoculars and now Michael is helping me to see it through the hubble telescope.

I can see how Michael has laid the perfect foundation for a beautiful flow of expansion, insights, and understanding from day one. It has helped me more easily get into a place of trusting and therefore allowing this process to unfold in the best possible way.

I have begun to feel a sort of flow that helps me stay more focused on what it is I want instead of what I don't, and that is a great feeling. I am also noticing that each day it becomes easier and easier to do so. I think what excites me the most is the fact that I am able to create this for myself. Through my pure desire it has come to be and that makes me feel good about me.

# Day 9 *March 21, 2011*

I DON'T KNOW WHAT it is about getting those light bulb moments while taking a shower, but this morning was a doozy. It is nothing short of a revelation how this journey has come in response to something more. Something broader, more far reaching and expansive than the handful of problem's in my life. It is also about addressing my desire to know how this spiritual/physical business works. I have spent years studying and seeking answers to life's dilemma's and it seems I should be doing a hell of a lot better with all that I know.

It seems like I have been on an endless quest to learn more because surely there must be more to know. There must be some holy grail of enlightenment that will make it all come together and make sense for me. As I am musing about all of this, suddenly Michael comes through with "there is nothing missing here". In an instant I experience a complete shift in perspective. It is like I have been given a magical elixir that has granted me absolute knowing that all I need or want is already within me.

Talk about liberating. All I can think is, halla-friggin-luya! As the full implication of what this truly means begins to set in, Michael's next words are music to my ears as well, "Simply claim it for yourself now". In other words, accept that what you want is there for the asking. Nothing is being withheld from you or not available to you. Believe it is already yours.

There seems to be a reoccurring theme here about our right to choose what we want and expect for ourselves. I am quite happy being reminded as often as I need to be. I feel that in lining up with this deceptively simple, yet powerful guidance, my life will be transformed.

# Day 10                          *March 22, 2011*

THIS MORNING I AM feeling wonderful, clear, and a sense of well-being that is almost intoxicating. I decide to take my happy little self out for a morning walk and go with the flow of this lovely state of being. Fortunately I live in somewhat of a rural area with plenty of sagebrush lined dirt roads away from everything so I can simply enjoy nature.

Here lately I have gotten into sort of a spontaneous rhythm where I leisurely stroll along until I feel inspired to pick up the pace and get a little cardio in. Then I pick a bush up ahead and jog to that point. I just mix it up as I go and never plan how much of one or the other I will do. It seems to always work out to be a perfectly balanced, very satisfying experience.

Today it is becoming even more so as I am seeing how much this little walk is a perfect metaphor on how to approach life. At the same time making me aware of how often I actually resist taking things a step at a time. I impatiently want to jump ahead so I can just get there, preferably the sooner the better. Usually afraid it may take too long, take forever, or god forbid, I won't get there at all.

As this whole scenario is playing out in my mind, I can almost sense Michael smiling playfully as the words "sometimes you gotta slow down to speed up" come into my mind. What a delightful way of showing me how I can incorporate something I am already doing to other aspects of my life. Not only achieving more of what I want, but through the path of least resistance. My walks will never be the same and in taking Michael's advice, neither will my life.

# Day 11                        *March 23, 2011*

I HAVE BEGUN WATCHING this show called "I survived beyond and back". It is about people who have had amazing near-death or actual-death experiences. There is not a whole lot on television that interests me, but I have really been drawn to this show and always feel inspired by it. It is clear that these people are experiencing what it is like from the non-physical or what is usually referred to as the other side.

Although each person has their own unique experience, there is one thing that is absolutely consistent in all of their stories. They all relate an indescribable sense of well-being, they feel loved and worthy beyond description, and any worries from life are insignificant and don't matter anymore. What does matter are the people in their lives, the joyful times, and wonderful experiences they have had. They all seem to come away from it with a different perspective that transforms how they look at life.

What is significant to me about it is, I have always felt that life could and should be more that way. It should be better, more fun, and a whole lot easier. It feels like I am being given validation in a way that it is possible. That I am attracting the things that support and confirm what I want, which is to live as the happy, joyful being I truly am.

Just as important I am seeing more and more how this law of attraction business really works. The better I am feeling and groovin along, the more is showing up in my experience to enhance and expand that state of being. It is becoming pretty obvious that my life isn't just randomly happening. I am attracting what is coming to me, every bit of it.

# Day 12                    *March 24, 2011*

I HAVE BARELY HAD my first cup of coffee when the words "it's not a big deal" come to me with a certainty that feels like I have merged with Michael's powerful knowing. It is instantly clear to me that creating anything we want is not the big deal we often make it out to be.

As my understanding expands I can see how I have been selectively putting the things I want into categories according to how easy or difficult I believe it will be to get them. With everything from Levis to the Lottery, I seem to have some level of expectation regarding my ability to have it. Basically it comes down to a belief that some things are harder to achieve than others. But now that seems like a tricky little trap I have set for myself that actually limits what I am able to receive.

The truth I see now, is that it is only our own idea or belief that some things are more difficult or a bigger deal than others. It is becoming pretty obvious to me that most of what we have been taught or lead to believe about getting what we want is actually opposite of how it really works. Being completely in sync with Michael's knowing makes that crystal clear. If you really think about it, the things you expect to be more difficult; are.

I guess the bottom line for me is, apparently I am the only one getting in my own way. But now with this understanding I can look at what I am wanting in a different way. I can let go of all the limiting thoughts usually attached to what I want and more purely line up with what I desire.

It is also occurring to me that I can ease up on making such a big deal about all the little annoying little things that come up throughout the day as well. I expect life will become easier, I will get more goodies and have a lot more fun in the process.

Thanks Michael

# Day 13 *March 25, 2011*

YESTERDAY AFTERNOON I HAD some unexpected feelings of self-doubt come over me regarding this experience I am having with Michael. I think they were coming up because a part of me is kind of surprised at how easy this seems to be. Isn't it interesting that even when we get something we want, especially something we consider extraordinary, we can still question it?

It didn't take long to figure out the no big deal insight not only provided guidance pertaining to my desires in general, but was helpful in regards to the self-doubt that showed up later as well. Obviously Michael knew the bigger picture and with flawless execution provided the perfect guidance to cover all of the bases for my greatest benefit.

Another great example to remind me that my needs are always understood and being addressed in ways I can't even conceive of sometimes. I also understand that because of the nature of this experience with the non-physical, some doubt was bound to creep in at some point. So at the end of the day I took Michael's advice and was able to see it is as not such a big deal and let it go. Kinda worked like magic......

There is one more aspect of this and that is when we are trying to change our usual habitual ways of thinking and doing things (which is what this is all about), our little minds are going to want to stick with the usual familiar program. We generally keep these habitual patterns because it feels safe and the minute we turn loose of what we perceive to be "our control" of the situation, we feel vulnerable.

We become so afraid that if we don't make a big deal about something, it will keep happening or possibly get worse. When actually what we are doing is putting more energy toward what we don't want which brings us more of just that because; what you resist persists. Changing habitual patterns is a bit like learning a different language, it just takes some practice. That is how we build the bridges that create change.

# Day 14                              *March 26, 2011*

I AM ALMOST IN awe of how effortless this has become as the knowing that "I am free" completely envelopes me this morning. A simple concept on it's own, but when Michael is involved it is a whole different ballgame. And oh boy is this one ever coming into focus for me. It is giving me a renewed awareness of the important role our thoughts play in this game of life.

Most of us have been conditioned to believe that it is our action that is responsible for creating. But that is like putting the cart before the horse, and once again we have got it backwards.

The truth is that everything begins with our thoughts; our mindset. Contrary to what some believe, we did not come into this life empty handed. We came fully equipped with the most important and powerful resource we could ever need; the freedom to choose our thoughts. That is the freedom Michael is referring to, and I can feel the huge significance of it.

I feel how truly empowering it is to KNOW that I am free. Free to believe what I chose, free to choose thoughts that are beneficial, not detrimental. Free to feel good regardless of what anyone else is choosing. Free to trust in a benevolent universe. Free to be whatever I want to be. FREE IN THE WAY THAT MATTERS MOST.

Just accepting that I am truly free feels so uplifting. It reminds me of the smile thing. Have you ever noticed that when you smile you seem to automatically feel good?

It's like some happy little chemical gets released in you. I am thinking the feeling I am having about being truly free is releasing that happy little chemical's, happy little cousin. And that is a very good thing.

# Day 15 *March 27, 2011*

AFTER THE "I AM free" reminder yesterday, I am feeling pretty fired up about my ability to create the changes I am wanting. I zero in on my partnership issue knowing that something has got to give.

I have been questioning whether or not we are even a good match anymore. This living with uncertainty business is just plain crappy. How I have been dealing with it is obviously not working. Trying to keep myself happy while feeling resentful towards my partner is like trying to ride two horses with one ass, not yielding the results I am after. You cannot experience happiness and resistance at the same time with any good results.

Thankfully a better understanding and approach reveals itself to me; I can drop my guarded position, relax about this, and let it be ok to get along. What a concept. I think I have been worried about sending the wrong message if I don't keep my guard up, when I am so unsure about the outcome of this relationship. But what that has done is perpetuate tension in the situation which seems so un-necessary to me now.

I realize I don't have to keep pushing against anything while I figure this out. It won't mean I am giving up what I want or settling in anyway, which has probably been one of my biggest fears. It actually means that I will experience a smoother and easier transition no matter what the outcome. It's called the path of least resistance. Maybe the change I am really needing, is in my own attitude and approach.

# Day 16                           *March 28, 2011*

I WAS THINKING ABOUT this habit I want to release and found myself instantly conjuring up all of the reasons it may be difficult to achieve. Then Michael comes through with "cut the dead weight from your desires". I immediately realize what I am doing at an almost unconscious level. Setting limits before I even get started, sabotaging myself right out of the gate. And I think, isn't it interesting that I am most prone to do this when it's something I really want?

I know that Michael is referring to more than just this habit issue. It's about all the ways we argue for our limitations, give in to self-defeating thoughts and beliefs, and talk ourselves right out of something based on some imaginary limits we have accepted as reality. Once again coming down to perception and habitual patterns of thinking which absolutely can be changed. So, even with something like a habit, a shift in perspective from looking at it as a potential struggle, to looking forward to the desired outcome makes all the difference.

I remember a few years ago, I was in line at a second hand shop when this little boy came bounding up to the counter with a skateboard in his arms asking his mom if he could have it. I could feel the excitement and pure desire he was radiating about this treasure he found. His mom said she would have to call his dad which I'm sure was her way of letting him down easy without saying no.

It actually didn't seem to dampen his spirit at all as he placed it carefully behind the counter with such certainty that it would be his. That is all it took because I already felt compelled to buy it for him and now there was no way I was going to let him leave there without it. I left there feeling so uplifted about how that little boy had not only just shown me, but inspired my participation in a beautiful example of how it's done.

# Day 17                    *March 29, 2011*

WITH THE GUIDANCE FROM yesterday still in mind, I am aware of another tendency I have in relation to my desires. It's about always wanting or needing evidence that it is or will be manifesting. It seems that implies a lot of doubt and if there is one thing I know, it is that doubt and manifesting are not compatible. I decide to ask Michael for help.

I am advised to let go of the notion that something is missing once again. A little dejavue here but I am sure it is needed. Then a further understanding opens up; when you cannot see the physical evidence, you tend to think there is something you might be missing. Maybe something that has been over looked, is incomplete, or left undone. That actually puts you in a place of not allowing it. The operative word to the universe (vibration) is MISSING.

It also sends the signal that you have not accepted that what you want is coming, if you are thinking or feeling something is lacking in the equation. It keeps what you want in sort of a holding pattern because you are not letting it in. It also ties in with a lack of trust and trying to control things, which who isn't guilty of?

You know when you are expecting an important call that hasn't come and you start wondering about all of the reasons that damn phone isn't ringing? Then you get sick of trying to figure it out and tired of waiting so you let it go. What happens; it rings. So the solution is to warm up to the idea that nothing is missing and everything is being taken care of, being arranged on your behalf, and in the process of happening. Relax and enjoy yourself in the meantime and watch what happens.

# Day 18                    *March 30, 2011*

I DON'T KNOW WHAT is happening here but I woke up feeling like some wild-fire breathing force of nature rose up in me and took over. Without hesitation, I lay out my frustrations and desires to Michael and ask for some big shift or turning point for myself, something significant to propel me forward.

Then I felt an overwhelming rush of emotion encompass me like a river pulling me under, and I surrendered. I went back to bed and said to Michael "I give up, I'm done. "All this stuff I have been wrestling with, I am ready to let it go". Well, that's all it took. As I lay there like a limp rag the tears begin to flow and turned into a deep sobbing that felt like it was coming from the depth of my being. It felt like deep rooted emotional energy was being triggered, brought up and pulled out of me.

An image came into my mind of my first husband who was killed when I was still pretty young. I got the sense that I was being released from any remaining trauma and grief from that experience. Then it let up briefly before happening once again. This time it was an image of my father who was very abusive. The same scenario occurred with the deep sobbing and releasing. Once again this happened, only this time it was in regard to my current partner with whom I have experienced a difficult journey (especially lately).

I didn't question this process, but allowed it knowing full well that something amazing and healing was going on here. I just accepted it as a beautiful gift from Michael and could feel with every molecule of my being Michael's love for me. I could feel the comfort, the kinship between us in a way that I cannot even describe with words. The love and appreciation was overwhelming. I could feel how Michael felt about me, and it was as pure divine beauty.

Then a calm and ease came over me that was so welcoming, I just melted into it. Then there were these pulsing sensations going on inside of my body like points of light being connected, one after another. It felt like I was being re-wired energetically. From being an energy worker myself, it was easy for me to intuit and understand to some degree. I knew this was something wonderful that was exactly what I had asked for.

Later that evening while I sat on my back porch, I wondered about the three experiences Michael had addressed. It suddenly came to me that those were the times in my life when I truly felt powerless. And with that understanding, I knew that this was a huge blessing.

# Day 19          *March 31, 2011*

I CANNOT BELIEVE THAT even after the amazing experience with Michael yesterday, I am having "am I imagining this" thoughts. It is especially surprising considering this isn't my first rodeo with out of the norm energy experiences. I decide to go for a walk and let it be while I wait for some clarity about it.

As I am cruising along it occurs to me, there is something in me holding on to the pre-conceived ideas about this experience with Michael; A very subtle internal struggle going on in my mind. Now I am really bewildered. A few moments later it comes over me; it's about control. It makes sense that having pre-conceived ideas of how something should go is actually a subtle form of trying to keep some kind of control, I get it.

Just when I think it is cleared up, the big light bulb moment comes when the words "survival mentality" light up my mind. A holy shit moment is there ever was one. It ties in perfectly with the powerless issue Michael addressed yesterday. All at once all of the dots are connecting that show how one state of being (survival mode) has a domino effect in so many ways.

It is all making sense how these habitual ways of thinking and doing things just take over. It's no wonder we can't understand why we keep getting what we are getting. Wow, it's like the sun just came out from behind the clouds allowing me to see in a new light.

# Day 20             *April 1, 2011*

IN WHAT FEELS LIKE the dynamic summary of the last couple of days, Michael is emphasizing that I am the one who holds the power to create my life. I am the most powerful person; it's me, I am it. I possess all of the potential I could possibly need within me. Now tell me, how many of us come close to believing that, much less know it about ourselves?

It is pretty obvious that I have somehow lost sight of the fact that I am the one in charge of my life. My only problem has been thinking that circumstances or other people have power over how my life plays out. The bottom line here is that somewhere along the way I have bought into the victim mentality, which has resulted in believing life is happening to me, instead of me making it happen.

What a difference a change in perception makes. The real brilliance in seeing it from Michael's perspective, is how detached I feel about goofing things up for myself. It actually is more like finally solving a mystery. It just feels liberating without any self-defeating side effects. It is pretty much a win/win situation.

The only word I can come up with to describe the incredible impact all of this is "sublime". It is a completely sublime orchestration on Michael's part, helping me beyond my wildest expectations. Out of curiosity I looked up the definition of sublime: exalted; lofty; majestic; supreme of the highest or noblest nature; awakening feelings of awe and veneration.

Yep, I picked the right word.

# Day 21                    *April 2, 2011*

I AM ACTUALLY BEING encouraged to play hookie today which totally delights the rebel in me. It seems like a good opportunity to take notice of how this adventure has already affected the general vibe of my life. Although nothing has been drastically or magically resolved, changes are happening. Everything is smoothing out and definitely moving in a more positive direction on all fronts as I am more able to maintain my balance regardless of circumstances.

Even those that I interact with seem to be catching a piece of the good vibes I am feeling now. When I call my mom (who is 83, by the way) I can hear the anticipation in her voice as the first thing she now asks is, what did you get from Michael today? I am always excited to share it with her and each time that I do I can tell the lights come on for her.

It is so rewarding when she tells me that she can see how it relates to something in her experience, maybe something she never even realized up to this point. I love that the tremendous benefit I am receiving is also of such value to her. It adds even more meaning to all of this. And it shows me that no matter how far along we are in life, we can learn ways to make it better. Everything I have asked for and more is happening and I can't wait for what's to come.

# Day 22 *April 3, 2011*

IT IS FUNNY HOW the more in the flow you are, the more the universe seems to playing your song. And it was literally a song coming on the radio while I was driving that gave me my next light bulb moment.

I can't even remember which song it was but I had a sudden understanding that I have been trying to be different. Doing what I thought were all the things to help me be a better version of myself. I have been trying to define myself by standards other than my own. Caring a little too much about how others perceive me as if there is some invisible list of expectations I need to live up to.

Regardless, a new light is shining for me now that feels like nothing but approval for who I am. And that my personality is my own unique expression in this world. Also that my personality (even the occasional cussing), is not the issue. It never has been. I am even seeing my rebel nature as an asset which makes me enjoy the fact even more that occasionally I kinda dig being a walking contradiction. Keeps em` guessing now doesn't it.

# Day 23                    *April 4, 2011*

MICHAEL IS HIGHLIGHTING THE tremendous value of consistency this morning. This is a biggie for me and probably one of my greatest challenges. I am so glad it is being addressed because I can feel how important it is.

It is really interesting to me that each time Michael presents guidance, I feel like I already know it but have been operating in some alternate universe that clouds the knowing. Right now it is clear as can be that when I remain consistent toward what is wanted, and not get off on Mr. Toad's wild ride when a challenge hits me, I can have what I want.

I am feeling so strongly that what I am wanting (whatever it may be) is always there for me. I suspect many times it has been right on the verge of happening had I stayed the course and remained true to my vision, my desire. I can see that there has never been a question of whether what I want is coming, it has been about allowing doubt to replace my expectation of it coming.

Maybe it comes down to trust, trusting that when I remain consistent with what I want instead of giving in to the self-defeating habit of putting my attention on what I don't want, I will reap the benefit. Yep, I have no doubt that is the point Michael is making. It seems I keep being reminded that this is a whole lot easier than we make it out to be.

# Day 24           *April 5, 2011*

WELL CRAP.......AFTER THAT GREAT insight about consistency yesterday sure enough one of those challenging situations came up and what did I do? Reverted right back to my habitual ways of responding and even had the nerve to ask Michael what the hell was going on. What did I get from Michael? Nothing, nada, seemingly dropped off my radar.

The computer in my bedroom did come on by itself in the middle of the night (which has happened several times since this began) reassuring me that I haven't really been abandoned. Almost as soon as I woke up this morning it comes to me that instead of getting worked up about what happened, I could have taken the opportunity to put into practice what Michael had advised.

As soon as I come to this awareness I sense that mischievous smile with the words "go with what you know". A gentle reminder that this isn't about Michael magically changing everything in my life, it's about offering the guidance and tools to do it for myself. It's about reassuring me that I am always heard, understood, and guided in ways that promote self-empowerment.

Even more, that the universe (or god, source, all that is or whatever you want to call it) is always offering assistance and support in so many ways. In the words of a song, some billboard with words that jump out at you, or something you hear at the moment you need it most. It is practically endless. I guess the moral of the story is to relax, trust, and pay attention because what you need will show up in one form or another.

# Day 25          *April 6, 2011*

I AM COMING TO the conclusion that there would be immense value and freedom for me in letting go of criticizing, blaming, or just plain feeling negativity towards others, particularly my partner. I have always loved the idea of being able to have a live and let live attitude toward everyone.

After I have a little chat with Michael about it I go take my shower and (big surprise) here it comes.....for as long as I can remember a big part of the way I have interacted with others (and my partner) has been what I now see clearly as a sort of trading game. An unspoken agreement, where we play the roles that we think are expected of us.

One example of this dynamic would be, how the one who brings in the most money (or all the money) holds an elevated position in a sort of invisible hierarchy, while the other person assumes a subtly more submissive position. In a nutshell, it usually comes down to the fact that I need to do things for you not necessarily because I want to but because you work harder and are bringing more to the table. I feel the need to justify my worthiness to receive something for not being the one who is the bread winner. I have been on both ends of this equation and neither one ever felt good to me.

I'm seeing it now as an imbalance of power because no matter which end of it you are on, you are not being true to yourself and therefor are out of touch with your own integrity. Sometimes that can get a little ugly and can create resentment, criticism and discontent. When you are out of balance with yourself it is so much easier to project criticism toward others and makes it really difficult to have a live and let live attitude.

When you are being true to yourself and living from a real sense of empowerment, you don't see others in a critical light. You see them and relate to them differently. As you withdraw from all of the little ways you barter away at pieces of yourself and reclaim who you really are, everything changes.

# Day 26                    *April 7, 2011*

I AM REVELING IN and marveling at this amazing journey this morning. As I do the words "it can just keep getting better" flow through my mind as if they were sprinkled with some magical fairy dust.

Then I feel it so completely. I am in the flow, totally and completely immersed in the flow of well-being and expansion. This is the good stuff that I have read and heard about and had many brief experiences of along the way. Now I know what all the hooplah is about. It rocks!

It doesn't feel anything like I have completed something and now I am good to go. Quite the contrary, it feels like riding and endless wave of possibilities, and an open-ended expansion that is life affirming and filled with ease. It takes away any sense of urgency and replaces it with eagerness. It feels like balance has settled into my soul and I am shining from the inside out.

# Day 27 *April 8, 2011*

I THINK IT IS good to not take ourselves too serious, to be able to laugh at ourselves and not worry about some of the crazy crap we do. I am getting a visual about those devices that set up an invisible perimeter to keep dogs contained. It teaches them to stay within the boundaries or they will get a good zapping.

Don't we do that to ourselves in a way? Set up our own self-imposed boundaries and limits from what we have been taught or lead to believe? Doesn't it take the fun out of life when we play it safe and stay within our own little comfort zones? Doesn't it take away our sense of adventure and our willingness to take chances? That is the crazy crap I am referring to.

Right now I am seeing the humor in all of it and it feels liberating. Each time I have received an insight from Michael, I have experienced a subsequent awareness of what I have been doing to hold myself back or create the problem. Not once have I felt any judgement, embarrassment, or self-criticism.

Quite the contrary, more often it feels like Michael and I are both having a good laugh at some of my antics. It has helped me see that I can be too hard on myself at times. We all can and it is just not necessary. Maybe we take all of this a bit too serious. So it is especially meaningful that Michael is accentuating the light-hearted aspect of all of this.

I am sure no matter how much we learn and grow, it wouldn't be nearly the ride it could be if we allowed ourselves a more light-hearted and playful attitude about it all.

# Day 28 *April 9, 2011*

As I am coming to the culmination of this extraordinary journey with Michael, I am almost overcome with appreciation. I had always thought I have been alone in my spiritual journey, since I didn't have a mentor or advisor to reach out to. I just tried to figure it out pretty much on my own. Now I see that nothing could be further from the truth.

Michael has helped me to realize and know that I have never been alone in this, none of us are. I am thinking about my loved ones, especially the women in my life. The strong, beautiful women whom I have shared my life. Who have loved me unconditionally no matter how far off the beaten path I have ventured. Who have most likely just shook their heads in amusement at my endless refusal to conform to anything considered ordinary.

They have been a source of love and support I am appreciating in a way I could have never imagined. I can feel the beauty of their souls and the grace of their presence in every moment of my life.

I couldn't have asked for more.

# Day 29                    *April 10, 2011*

VERY POWERFULLY, THE MESSAGE is "there is no failure in life". I have got the feeling that Michael is leading up to something and I think it is about taking this beyond something for just my own benefit. It has occurred to me a few times along the way, that I could share this gift with others, especially the day I received the Hay House Publishing email. For now I will just go with the flow and see what happens.

From the broader perspective there is no such thing as failure. It is an illusion. To be afraid of what we perceive as failure is to be afraid to live. I ask Michael to give me a new interpretation on the idea of failure. The response is; opportunity in disguise. Ok, now the lights are coming on.

This is how I have felt stuck so many times before. I would talk myself into believing the reason I didn't try something was because maybe I wasn't qualified, or the timing wasn't right. There never has been a shortage of excuses for why I couldn't.

I do believe that Michael is alluding to the fact (in the most light-hearted way of course) that I can be a bit of a chicken shit, secretly afraid to fail; Gotta love it. I am being reminded that many times what I thought was a wrong move or failure, actually lead me to something better.

Then there is the not wanting to look bad or like a failure in other people's eyes baloney I have been guilty of. I will say there have been times when I was scared, even intimidated, but I did it anyway. When part of me knew it was a good thing, something I wanted, so I mustered up the courage to do it anyway. Looking back, it never turned out to be the big deal I had made it out in my mind.

It reminds me of the first job I got driving an 18 wheeler. When I got behind the steering wheel I was nervous as hell, but I wanted to do it so badly I just put it in gear and headed down the road. I took to it like a duck to water. It also turned out to be one of the most empowering things I have ever done.

I do believe I have got the point Michael.

# Day 30                    *April 11, 2011*

THE FEELING IS A little bittersweet this morning knowing it is the last day of this wonderful adventure. There is not much doubt from the direction this took yesterday that the idea of this becoming a book could be a reality. On this last day I am still amazed at how Michael had a bigger picture in mind, knowing I have always wanted to write a book that would be helpful and inspiring to others. It is delightfully ironic that something I began to seek help for myself, would end up being just that.

I have always enjoyed drawing so I start thinking about what kind of artwork I could do for a cover design. I'm lost in thought when Michael relates that I will have to be serious about this if I want to do it. After the way this has gone with the idea of relaxing, trusting, and not taking things too seriously it seems contradictory and frankly surprises the hell out of me. I don't get it because the idea of being serious feels heavy, burdensome, and almost counter-intuitive.

It takes a while but I settle down about it and trust once more that it will come together and make sense. And then it does, big time. The first thing coming through is that I have had a real tendency to be complacent, especially here lately in my life. I have somehow almost completely lost the passion and drive behind my dreams. I have settled into a kind of inertia about it all. There is an old school word for it and it's called "lollygagging".

What I am feeling from Michael's perspective is a different aspect of serious. It is more as in meaning it.

Deciding that it will be and getting serious in a beneficial way that projects an intentional energy; ok now were talking. Seeing it in this way, I can relate as I remember the times when I got down right serious about something and felt pretty darn unstoppable as a result. I understand completely now. I have been given what I needed every step of the way and today is no exception. I have loved and enjoyed this journey with Michael beyond words. I no longer feel as though something is ending, I think it's just the beginning.

Thank you Michael, from the deepest place in my heart.

# One more thing

THE DAY AFTER I finished this journey with Michael, something happened that is definitely worth mentioning. I was talking to my mom about this experience with Michael and she mentioned a remark that a family member had made about it. I was a bit blind-sided when she said that they were skeptical that I was interacting with Archangel Michael.

I guess it never occurred to me that anyone that knows me would have any doubt. I was surprised and offended. Even though I knew better, I let it get under my skin and it ticked me off. I decided to ask Michael for a sign, something tangible that would give me some kind of proof.

On one hand it felt like I was invalidating what I absolutely knew to be true. But on the other hand, I had a feeling that it may turn out to be a good thing somehow. Without hesitation, Michael let me know that white feathers would be my sign. I found that interesting since feathers showing up has always been like a sign to me.

The rest of the day went by without anything happening. But that night I had a lucid dream (the kind where you aware that you are dreaming) where I was walking along in nature and all of a sudden there were these giant 6 ft. long feathers laying across the path in front of me. I knew it was my sign and literally jumped for joy in my dream.

I woke up the next morning feeling so appreciative that Michael had done this for me. In doing so, I was given so much more. I was given something that would forever establish complete trust within myself, and my experiences. That means everything to me, and in an interesting sort of way, I got the extraordinary ending I was secretly hoping for.

# Afterword

I REMEMBER THE FIRST time I heard the expression "anything is possible". A part of me believed it could be true. Now I know it is. I am eternally grateful to Michael for that. I am also proud of myself for following the inspiration to take this journey.

What I have received has been far beyond what I could have imagined. Questions were answered in ways that completely surprised and delighted me. Some days it felt like I was dipped in magic waters that were cleansing my soul. I was thrilled when I began to realize that the insights I received could be beneficial to others as well. There is nothing I love more than sharing what I call "the good stuff" with others.

Everything I wanted to know about how to apply the law of attraction to my life circumstances was given. I am still a bit spellbound about the ways in which Michael helped me. I think the greatest thing I received from Michael was empowerment. Giving me back my power, and helping me to reclaim it for myself.

That is huge because I think we all get a little lost, vulnerable, and just plain whipped along the way. So much so that we tend to lose sight of who we really are. So being reminded of my strength, worthiness, and divinity is priceless.

Any doubts I may have had about being the creator of my life have vanished. I will admit that up until now

I have been half-hearted about stepping up and being a deliberate creator in my life. But now all I see are possibilities. I know that it is not only my responsibility, but a priveledge, to take charge of creating the life I want. Because after all, I am the one who will be living it.